The scriptures in this book are from various biblical translations.

For permission requests, contact Forever Open Journal & Notebook Collection and Dr. Shavon Leach at foreveropenjn@gmail.com.

Published in North Carolina by Forever Open Journal & Notebook Collection LLC and Dr. Shavon Leach.

Forever Open Journal & Notebook Collection LLC
Foreveropenjn.com

I0559146

Commit your actions to the Lord, and your plans will succeed. Pro. 16:3

TABLE OF CONTENTS

Proverbs 16:3
New Living Translation
Commit your actions to the Lord,
and your plans will succeed.

Purpose Affirmation

I am uniquely created and equipped to fulfill the purpose God has set for me.

How does this make you feel?

What does this mean to you?

How will this affirmation transform you?

Section 1
My God-given Purpose

A woman of purpose is a woman on a mission to filfull God's purpose in her life. She wants to make a difference, to create change, and to build a path that leads others to God. A woman of purpose is not defined in a single statement. A woman of purpose is:

A healer

A leader

A supporter

A mother

A sister

A aunt

A friend

A teacher

A business owner

A risk taker

A provider

A counselor

A blessing

A prayer warrior

She is whoever God has called her to be!

My God-given Purpose
Reflection

How has your faith journey influenced your understanding of your God-given purpose?

What specific talents or gifts do you believe God has given you, and how do you plan to use them?

What scriptures and biblical principles guides you in your purpose?

How do you seek God's guidance and discern His will for your life?

How will you overcome the enemy's traps and schemes so you can fulfill your God-given purpose?

How will you measure progress and success in fulfilling your God-given purpose?

In what ways will you incorporate discipleship into your God-given purpose?

Embracing your purpose allows you to step into your greatest potential. Embracing your purpose is not only for yourself. Your life is meant to impact those around you. Some ways to embrace your purpose are:

1. Take healthy risks.
2. Step outside of your comfort zone.
3. Work from your heart.
4. Use your failures as a lesson.

Woman of Purpose Qualities

Love (Agape) - John 13:34-35

Joy - Philippians 4:4

Peace - Colossians 3:15

Patience - Ephesians 4:2

Kindness - Galatians 5:22

Goodness - Romans 12:9

Faithfulness - 1 Corinthians 4:2

Gentleness - Philippians 4:5

Self-Control - 2 Peter 1:5-6

Humility - Philippians 2:3-4

Forgiveness - Colossians 3:13

Compassion - Ephesians 4:32

Integrity - Proverbs 10:9

Honesty - Proverbs 12:22

Generosity - 2 Corinthians 9:6-7

Diligence - Proverbs 13:4

Wisdom - James 1:5

Gratitude - 1 Thessalonians 5:18

Hope - Romans 15:13

Faith - Hebrews 11:1

Obedience - John 14:15

Righteousness - Matthew 5:6

Purity - Matthew 5:8

Peace-making - Matthew 5:9

Meekness - Matthew 5:5

Servanthood - Mark 10:45

Holiness - 1 Peter 1:16

Loyalty - Proverbs 17:17

Perseverance - James 1:12

Modesty - 1 Timothy 2:9

Accountability - James 5:16

Responsibility - Galatians 6:5

Truthfulness - Ephesians 4:25

Prayerfulness - Colossians 4:2

Sobriety - 1 Peter 5:8

Contentment - Philippians 4:11-13

Sincerity - 2 Corinthians 1:12

Endurance - 2 Timothy 4:7

Courage - Joshua 1:9

Reverence - Proverbs 1:7

Stewardship - 1 Peter 4:10

Empathy - Romans 12:15

Sacrifice - Romans 12:1

Discipline - 1 Corinthians 9:27

Unity - Ephesians 4:3

Temperance - Titus 2:2

Rejoicing in suffering - Romans 5:3-5

Boldness in witness - Acts 4:29

What qualities do you struggle with? Why? And how will you surrender to God so he can grow these qualities in you?

Commit your actions to the Lord, and your plans will succeed. Pro. 16:3

Positive Affirmation

With God's guidance and strength, I am empowered to make a positive impact and live out my purpose, bringing light and love to those around me.

How does this make you feel?

What does this mean to you?

How will this affirmation transform you?

Section 2
My God-given Purpose Plan

Mission

A mission is a short statement about why you are doing what you are doing and your overall goal.

What is your mission?

Vision

A vision is a short, simple, clear, and concise statement that is inspirational and paints a picture of the future.

Picture It!

What do you see when you think about your purpose?

Drawings and ideas of what God has shown you

Use this space to write your vision statement:

Goals & Objectives

Goals

Goals are what you want to achieve. When developing your goals make sure they are SMART.

Specific - Focused, Simple, Relevant.

Measurable - Clear, how much, how many, how it is going to happen.

Attainable - Reasonable, you do not have to jump through magical hoops to complete your goals.

Realistic - Inline with your values and goals.

Timely - The specific " when " goals will be completed.

Objectives

Objectives are developed from goals. Objectives are specific steps to take to reach your goals. Think about how you are going to make your mission and vision a reality.

Goals can have more than one objective.

My Goals & Objectives

Write out your goal and objectives for your purpose.

Goal

Objectives

1.

2.

3.

Goal

Objectives

1.

2.

3.

Goal

Objectives

1.

2.

3.

Goal

Objectives

1.

2.

3.

Goal

Objectives

1.

2.

3.

Purpose Audience

Your purpose audience is the people that God has called you to impact. Things to consider when thinking about your purpose audience are demographics such as:

- age
- gender
- location
- income
- education
- background
- marital/family status
- etc.

You may also want to consider psychographics such as:

- personality
- attitude
- values
- interest
- lifestyle
- etc.

Who is your purpose audience? What demographics and psychographics are important to your God-given purpose?

Resources

What resources do you need? And Why? (ex: email platform, funds, marketing firm, etc.)

Who do you need? And why? (ex: partnerships, employees, etc.)

My Purpose S.A.F.E Analysis

A SAFE analysis is a strategic planning tool used to identify how you will serve, your God-given authority, your faithfulness, and your effectiveness.

Serve- How will you serve? What are you going to do?.

My Purpose S.A.F.E. Analysis

Authority-how are you going to use your god-given authority?

My Purpose S.A.F.E Analysis

Faithfulness-What are you going to do remain faithful to God and the purpose he has given you?

My Purpose S.A.F.E Analysis

Effective-How are you going to effectively fulfill your God-given purpose?

Projected Annual Budget

The purpose of a projected annual budget is to project your income and expenses for a 12-month period.

Your income is anything that generates revenue, for example, sales, and your expenses are anything that costs you, for example, business travel.

Developing a projected annual budget is crucial to the success of your God-given purpose as it will help you balance and stay on top of your financial activities for the year.

Use the next page to help you develop your projected budget

Project Annual Budget Template

The projected column is what you expected your income and expenses to be.
The actual column is the accurate amount of your income and expenses .

Income	Projected	Total	Actual	Total
Sales				
Individual Contributions/ Investments				
Business Grants				
Others:				
Others:				
Others:				
	Total:	Total:	Total:	Total:
Expenses	Projected	Total	Actual	Total
Accounting				
Advertising				
Bookkeeper				
Fees & Subscriptions				
Insurance				
Internet				
Legal				
Maintenance & Repairs				
Office Supplies				
Payroll				
Phone Service				
Printing & Mailing				
Rent or Mortgage				
Taxes & Licenses				
Travel				
Training & Development				
Utilities				
Web Hosting & Domain				
Others:				
Others:				
Others:				
Others:				
Others:				
	Total:	Total:	Total:	Total:

My God-given Purpose Plan

Mission

Vision

Goals

Objectives

Target Audience

Resources

S.A.F.E

Annual Projected Budget

Use the next several pages to

combine all the pieces of your plan.

Project Annual Budget Template

Income	Projected	Total	Actual	Total
Sales				
Individual Contributions/ Investments				
Business Grants				
Others:				
Others:				
Others:				
	Total:	Total:	Total:	Total:
Expenses	**Projected**	**Total**	**Actual**	**Total**
Accounting				
Advertising				
Bookkeeper				
Fees & Subscriptions				
Insurance				
Internet				
Legal				
Maintenance & Repairs				
Office Supplies				
Payroll				
Phone Service				
Printing & Mailing				
Rent or Mortgage				
Taxes & Licenses				
Travel				
Training & Development				
Utilities				
Web Hosting & Domain				
Others:				
Others:				
Others:				
Others:				
Others:				
	Total:	Total:	Total:	Total:

Section 3
Woman of Purpose Planner

Intentions For The Week

SUNDAY

MONDAY

TUESDAY

WEDNESDAY

THURSDAY

FRIDAY

SATURDAY

notes

Week of

Habit Tracker: Week_____

Use this page to track your habits for the week as you are working to fulfill your God-given purpose.

	S	M	T	W	T	F	S
_____							
_____							
_____							
_____							
_____							
_____							
_____							
_____							
_____							

Date: _____

Goal Of the Meeting

Discussion Items

Attendees

Action Items/ Follow Up

Meeting

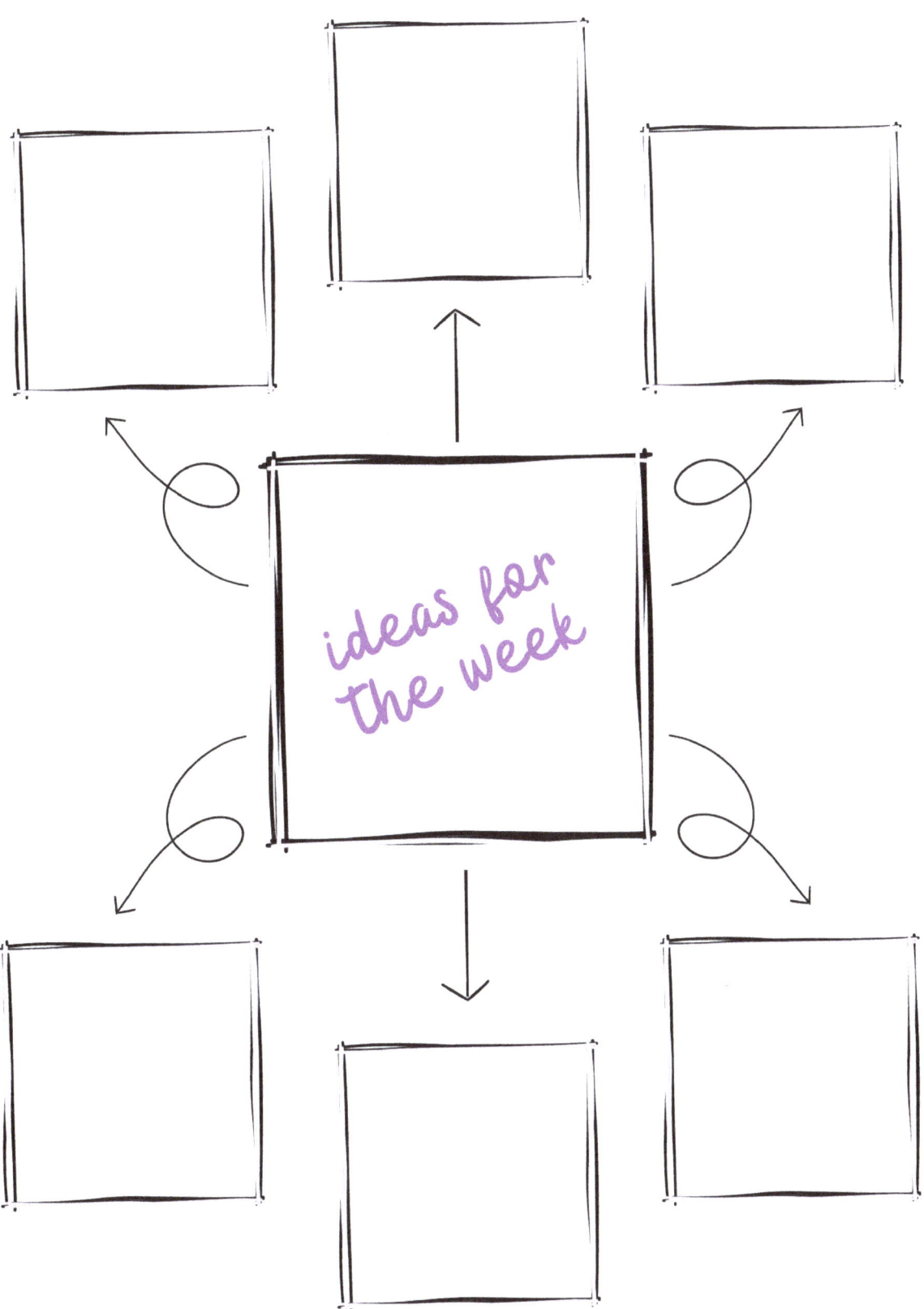

ideas for the week

Intentions For The Week

SUNDAY

MONDAY

TUESDAY

WEDNESDAY

THURSDAY

FRIDAY

SATURDAY

notes

Week of

Habit Tracker: Week_____

Use this page to track your habits for the week as you are working to fulfill your God-given purpose.

S   M   T   W   T   F   S

_____

_____

_____

_____

_____

_____

_____

_____

_____

Date: _____

Goal Of the Meeting

Discussion Items

Attendees

Action Items/ Follow Up

Meeting

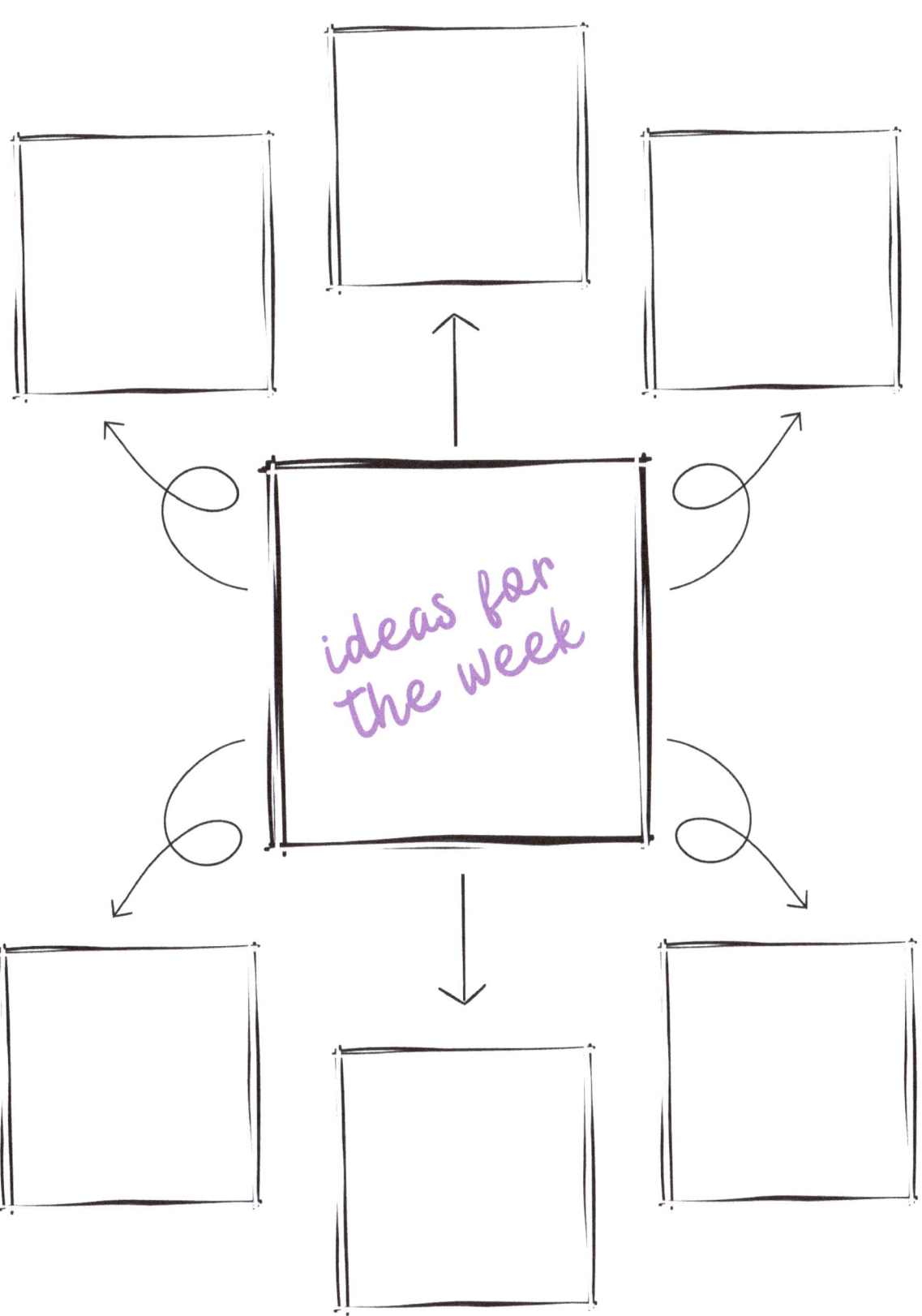

ideas for the week

Intentions For The Week

SUNDAY

MONDAY

TUESDAY

WEDNESDAY

THURSDAY

FRIDAY

SATURDAY

notes

Week of _____

Habit Tracker: Week_____

Use this page to track your habits for the week as you are working to fulfill your God-given purpose.

S   M   T   W   T   F   S

_____

_____

_____

_____

_____

_____

_____

_____

_____

Date: _____

Goal Of the Meeting

Discussion Items

Attendees

Action Items/ Follow Up

Notes

Meeting

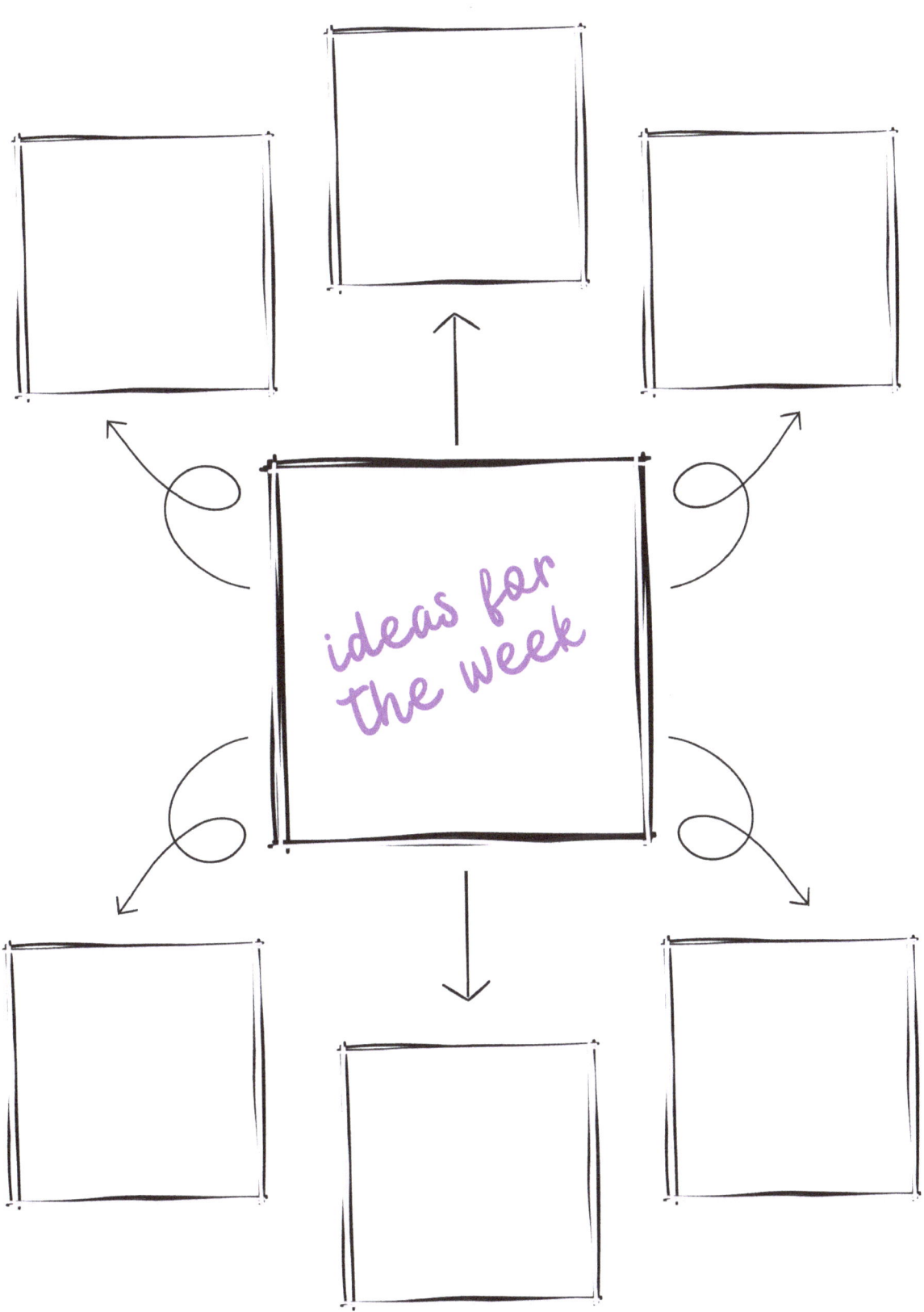

ideas for the week

Intentions For The Week

SUNDAY

MONDAY

TUESDAY

WEDNESDAY

THURSDAY

FRIDAY

SATURDAY

notes

Week of _____

Habit Tracker: Week_____

Use this page to track your habits for the week as you are working to fulfill your God-given purpose.

                                 S   M   T   W   T   F   S

Date: _____

Goal Of the Meeting

Discussion Items

Attendees

Meeting

Action Items/ Follow Up

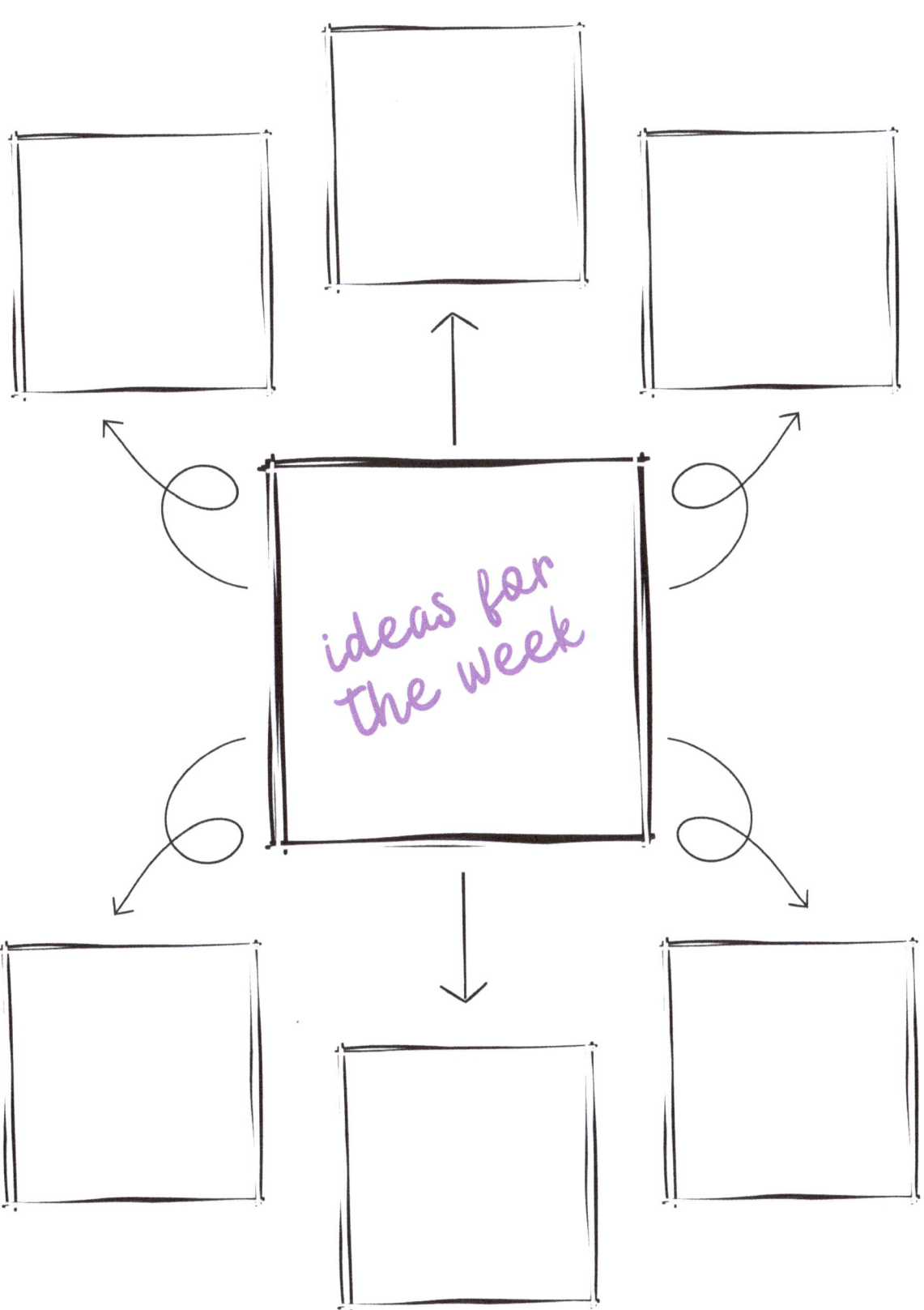

ideas for the week

Intentions For The Week

SUNDAY

MONDAY

TUESDAY

WEDNESDAY

THURSDAY

FRIDAY

SATURDAY

notes

Week of _____

Habit Tracker: Week _____

Use this page to track your habits for the week as you are working to fulfill your God-given purpose.

	S	M	T	W	T	F	S
_____							
_____							
_____							
_____							
_____							
_____							
_____							
_____							
_____							
_____							

Date: _____

Goal Of the Meeting

Discussion Items

Attendees

Action Items/ Follow Up

Meeting

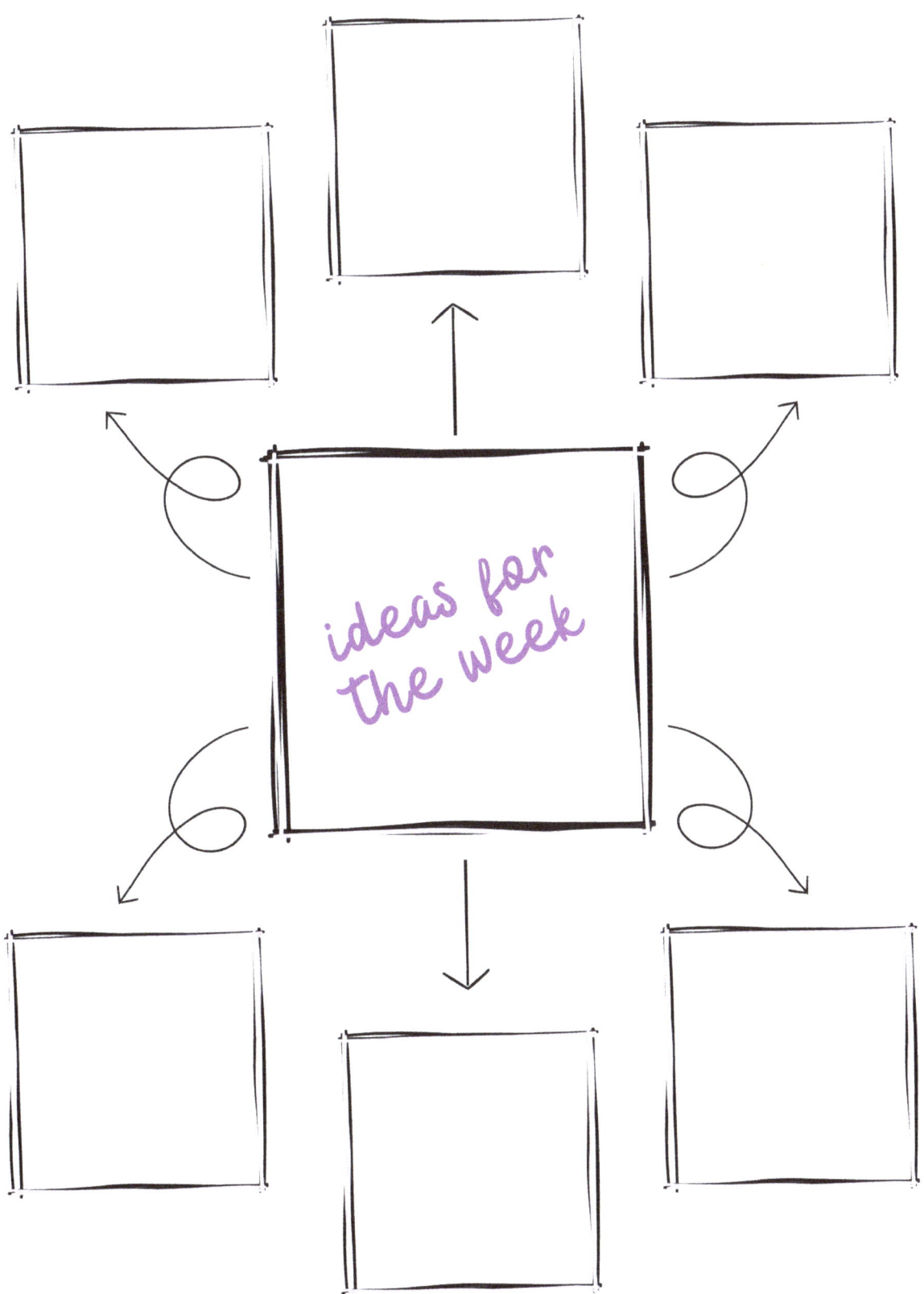

ideas for the week

Intentions For The Week

SUNDAY

MONDAY

TUESDAY

WEDNESDAY

THURSDAY

FRIDAY

SATURDAY

notes

Week of

Habit Tracker: Week_____

Use this page to track your habits for the week as you are working to fulfill your God-given purpose.

S   M   T   W   T   F   S

_____

_____

_____

_____

_____

_____

_____

_____

_____

Date: _____

Goal Of the Meeting

Discussion Items

Attendees

Action Items/ Follow Up

Meeting

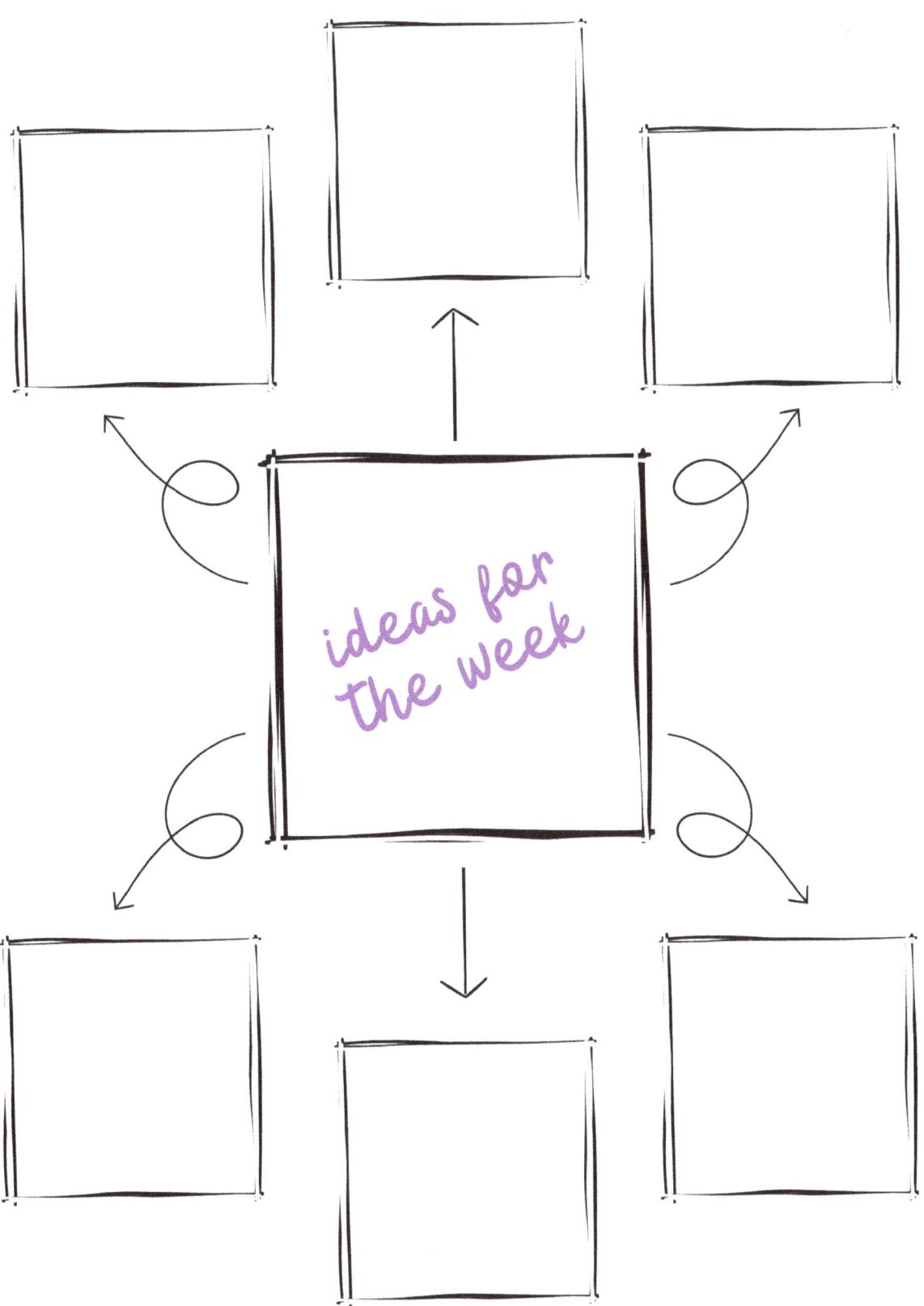

ideas for the week

Intentions For The Week

SUNDAY

MONDAY

TUESDAY

WEDNESDAY

THURSDAY

FRIDAY

SATURDAY

notes

Week of

Habit Tracker: Week_____

Use this page to track your habits for the week as you are working to fulfill your God-given purpose.

	S	M	T	W	T	F	S
_____							
_____							
_____							
_____							
_____							
_____							
_____							
_____							
_____							

Date: _____

Goal Of the Meeting

Discussion Items

Attendees

Action Items/ Follow Up

Meeting

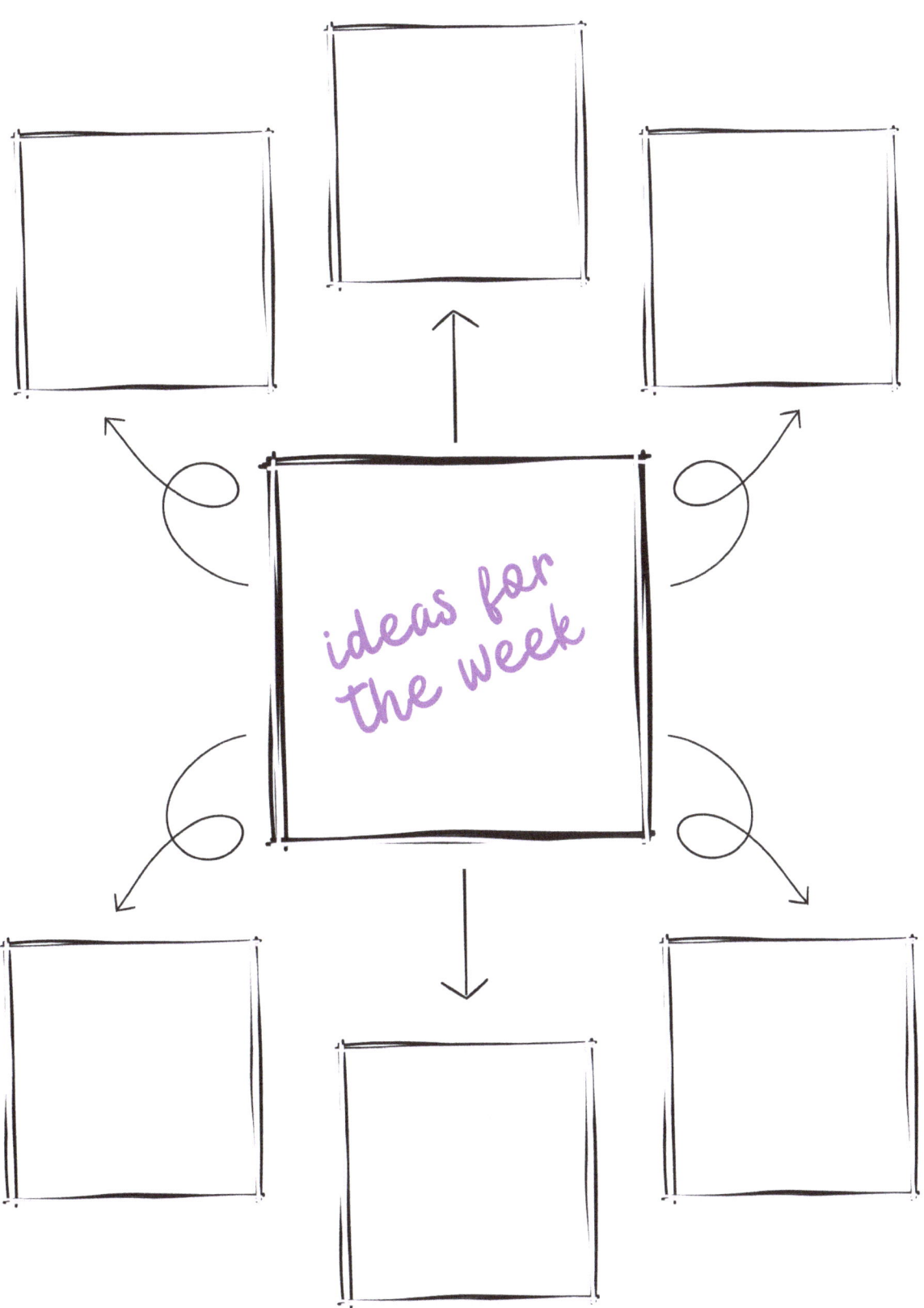

ideas for the week

Intentions For The Week

SUNDAY

MONDAY

TUESDAY

WEDNESDAY

THURSDAY

FRIDAY

SATURDAY

notes

Week of _____

Habit Tracker: Week _____

Use this page to track your habits for the week as you are working to fulfill your God-given purpose.

S   M   T   W   T   F   S

_____

_____

_____

_____

_____

_____

_____

_____

_____

_____

Date: _____

Goal Of the Meeting

Discussion Items

Attendees

Meeting

Action Items/ Follow Up

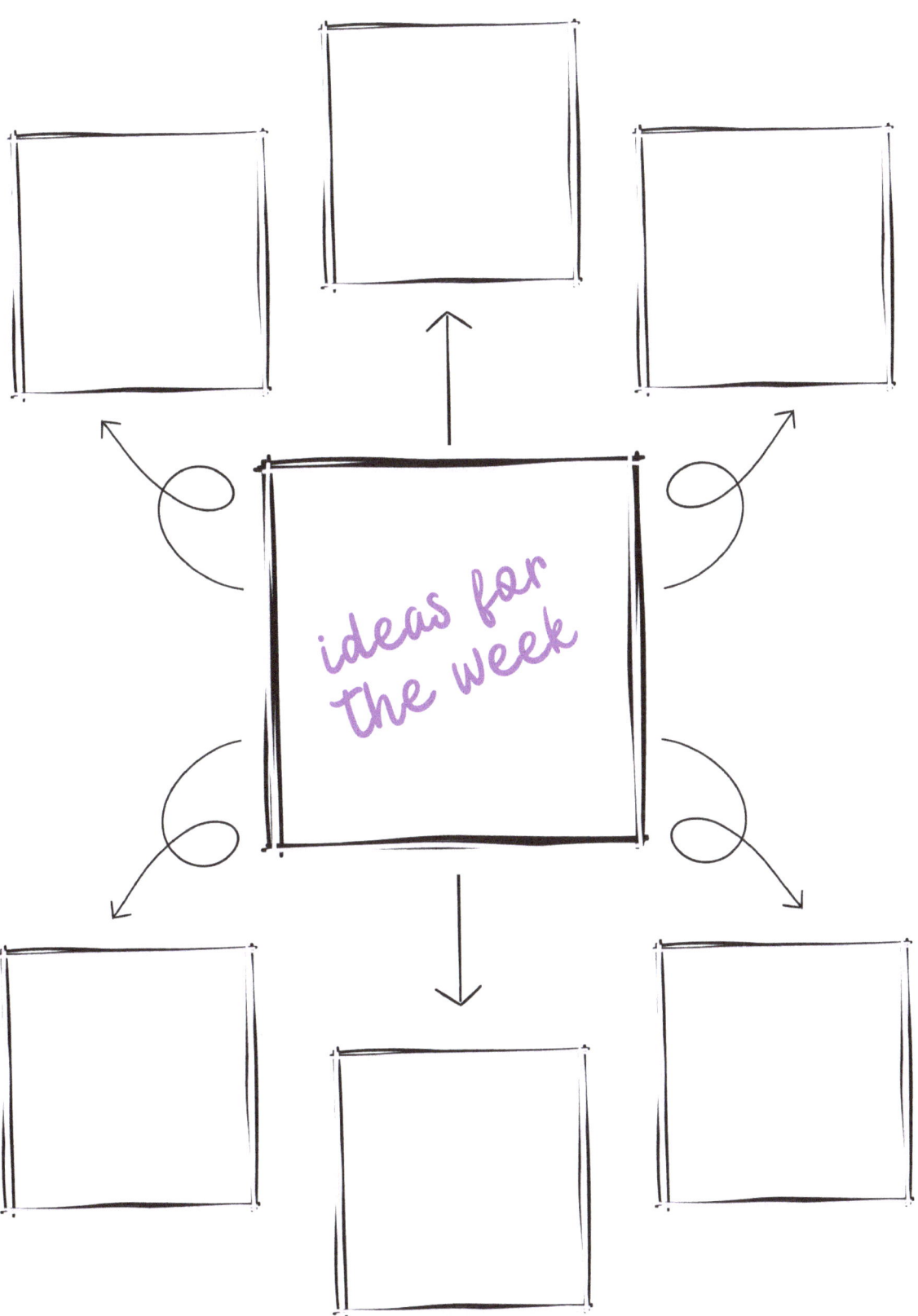

ideas for the week

Intentions For The Week

SUNDAY

MONDAY

TUESDAY

WEDNESDAY

THURSDAY

FRIDAY

SATURDAY

notes

Week of

Habit Tracker: Week_____

Use this page to track your habits for the week as you are working to fulfill your God-given purpose.

                        S   M   T   W   T   F   S

_____

_____

_____

_____

_____

_____

_____

_____

_____

Date: _____

Goal Of the Meeting

Discussion Items

Attendees

Action Items/ Follow Up

Meeting

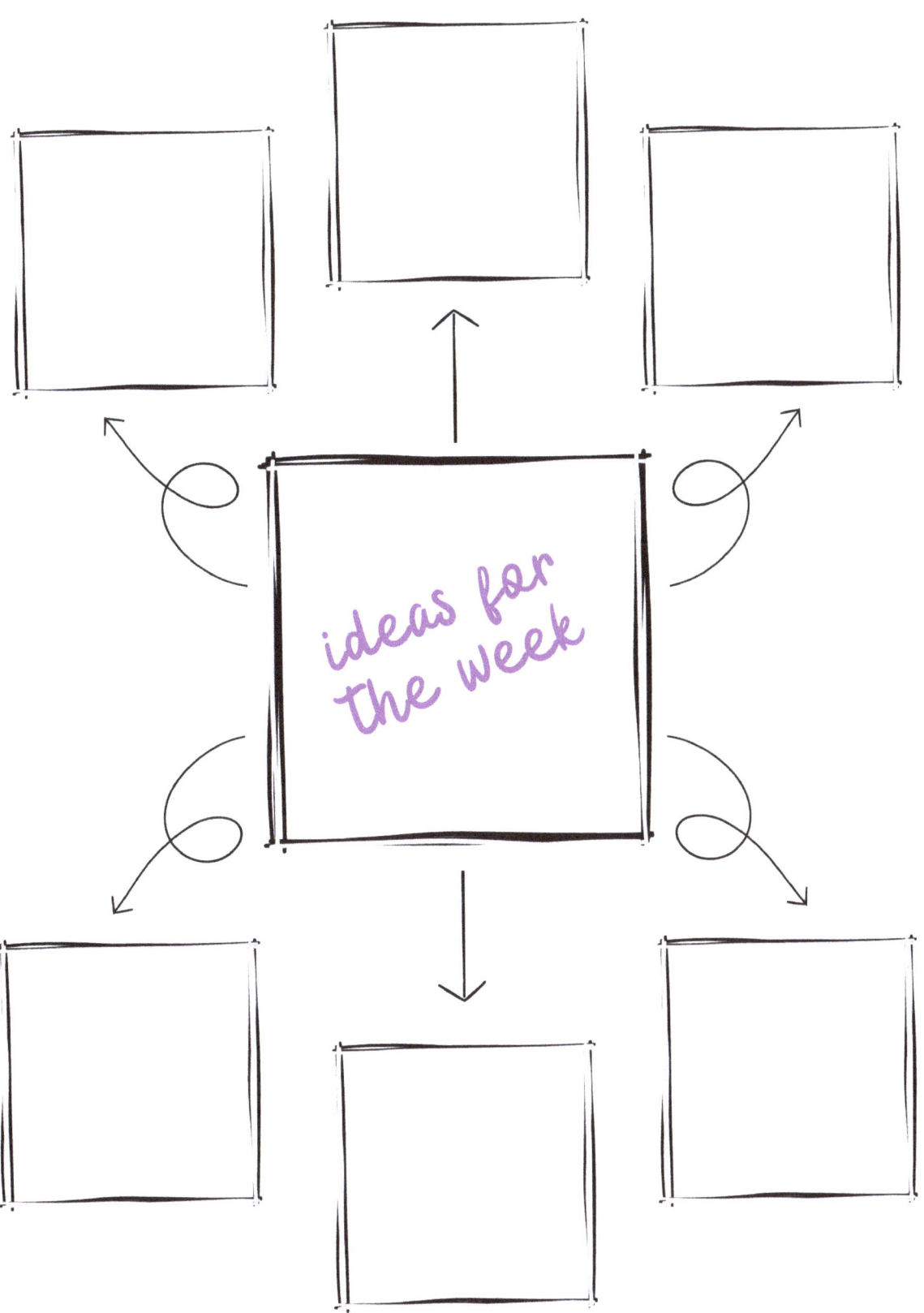

ideas for the week

Intentions For The Week

SUNDAY

MONDAY

TUESDAY

WEDNESDAY

THURSDAY

FRIDAY

SATURDAY

notes

Week of ------------

Habit Tracker: Week_____

Use this page to track your habits for the week as you are working to fulfill your God-given purpose.

                    S   M   T   W   T   F   S

_____

_____

_____

_____

_____

_____

_____

_____

_____

_____

Date: _____

Goal Of the Meeting

Discussion Items

Attendees

Action Items/ Follow Up

Notes

Meeting

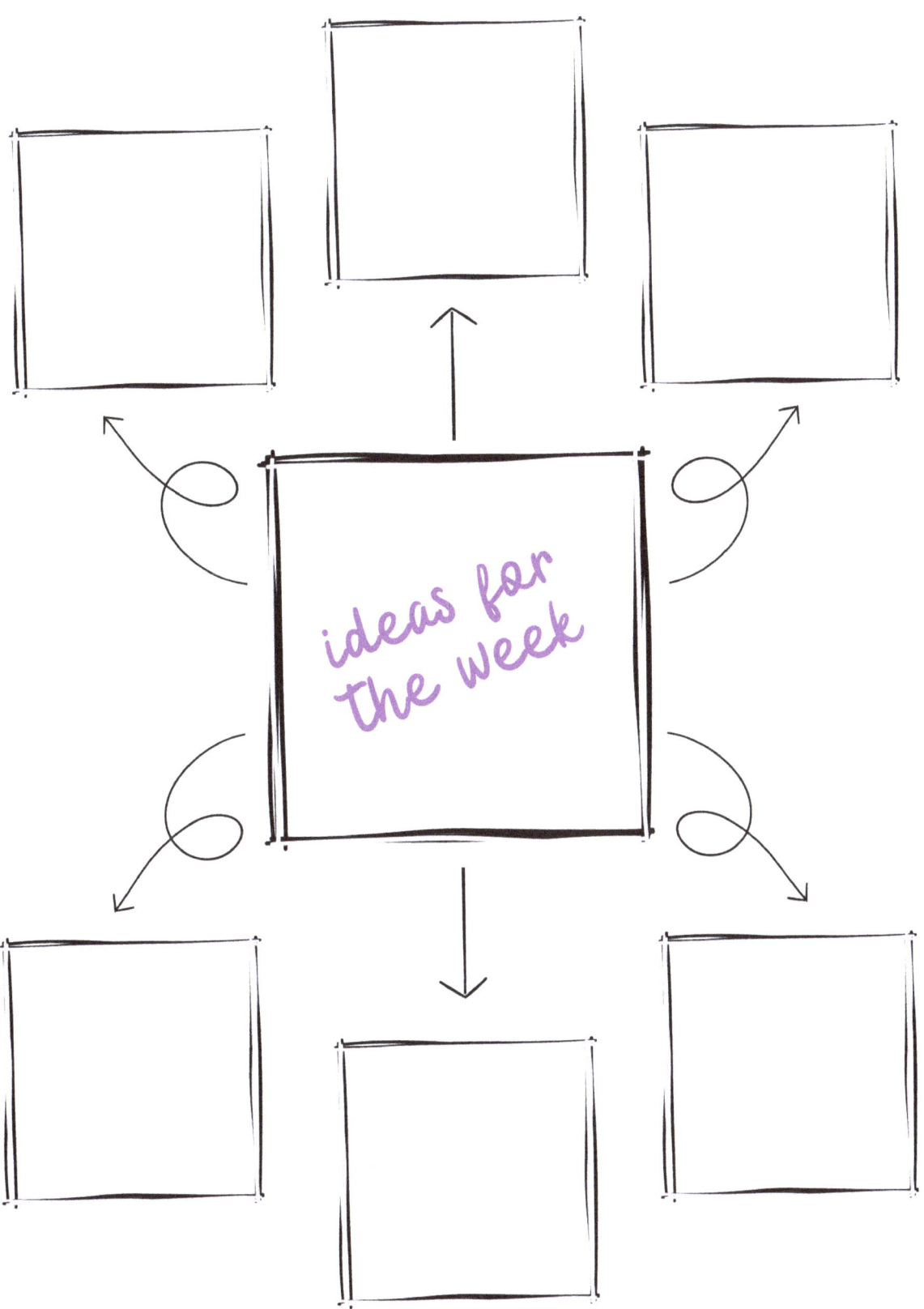

ideas for the week

Intentions For The Week

SUNDAY

MONDAY

TUESDAY

WEDNESDAY

THURSDAY

FRIDAY

SATURDAY

notes

Week of ----------

Habit Tracker: Week_____

Use this page to track your habits for the week as you are working to fulfill your God-given purpose.

	S	M	T	W	T	F	S

Date: _____

Goal Of the Meeting

Discussion Items

Attendees

Action Items/ Follow Up

Notes

Meeting

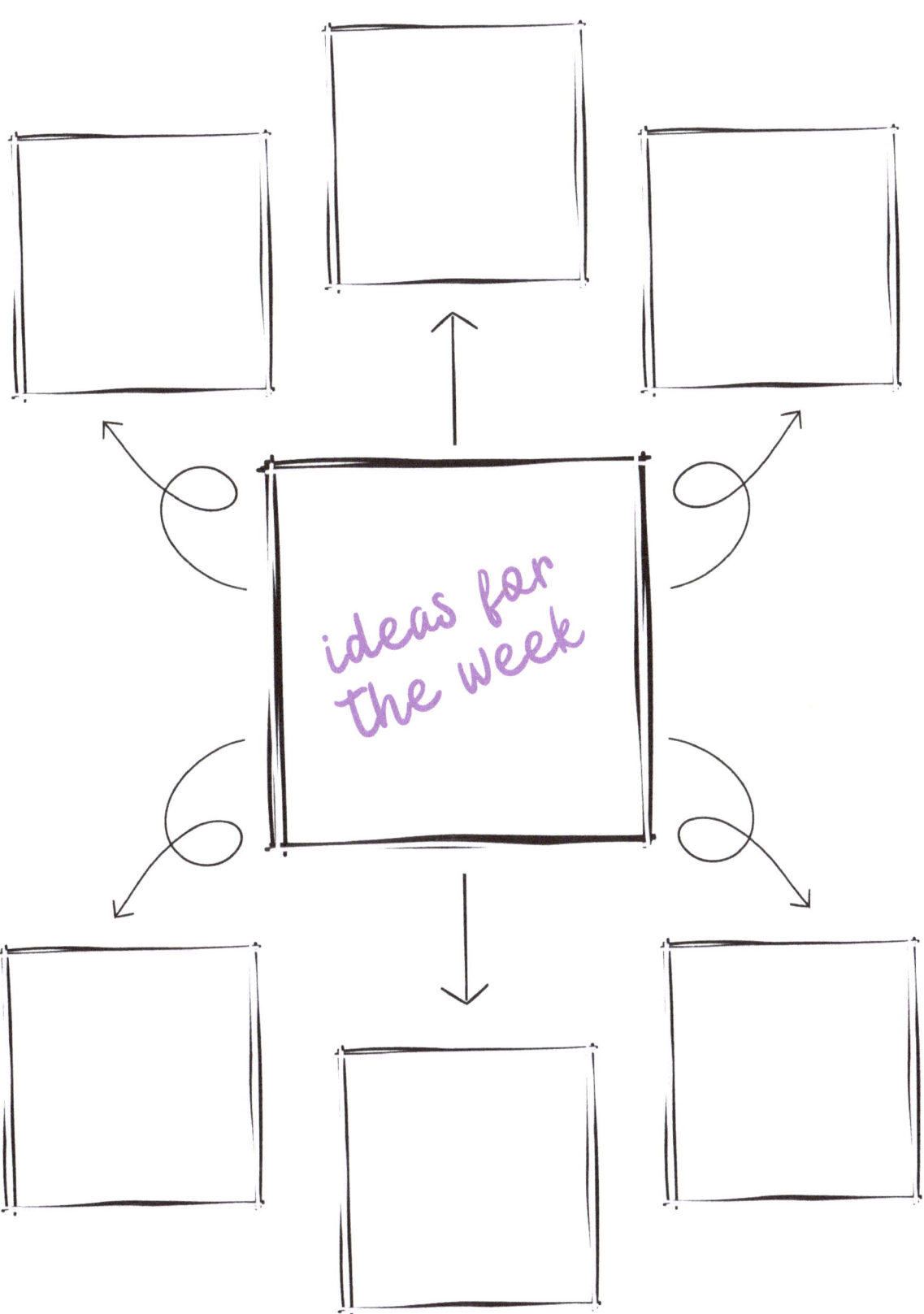

ideas for the week

Intentions For The Week

SUNDAY

MONDAY

TUESDAY

WEDNESDAY

THURSDAY

FRIDAY

SATURDAY

notes

Week of

Habit Tracker: Week_____

Use this page to track your habits for the week as you are working to fulfill your God-given purpose.

S   M   T   W   T   F   S

_____

_____

_____

_____

_____

_____

_____

_____

_____

_____

Date: _____

Goal Of the Meeting

Discussion Items

Attendees

Action Items/ Follow Up

Notes

Meeting

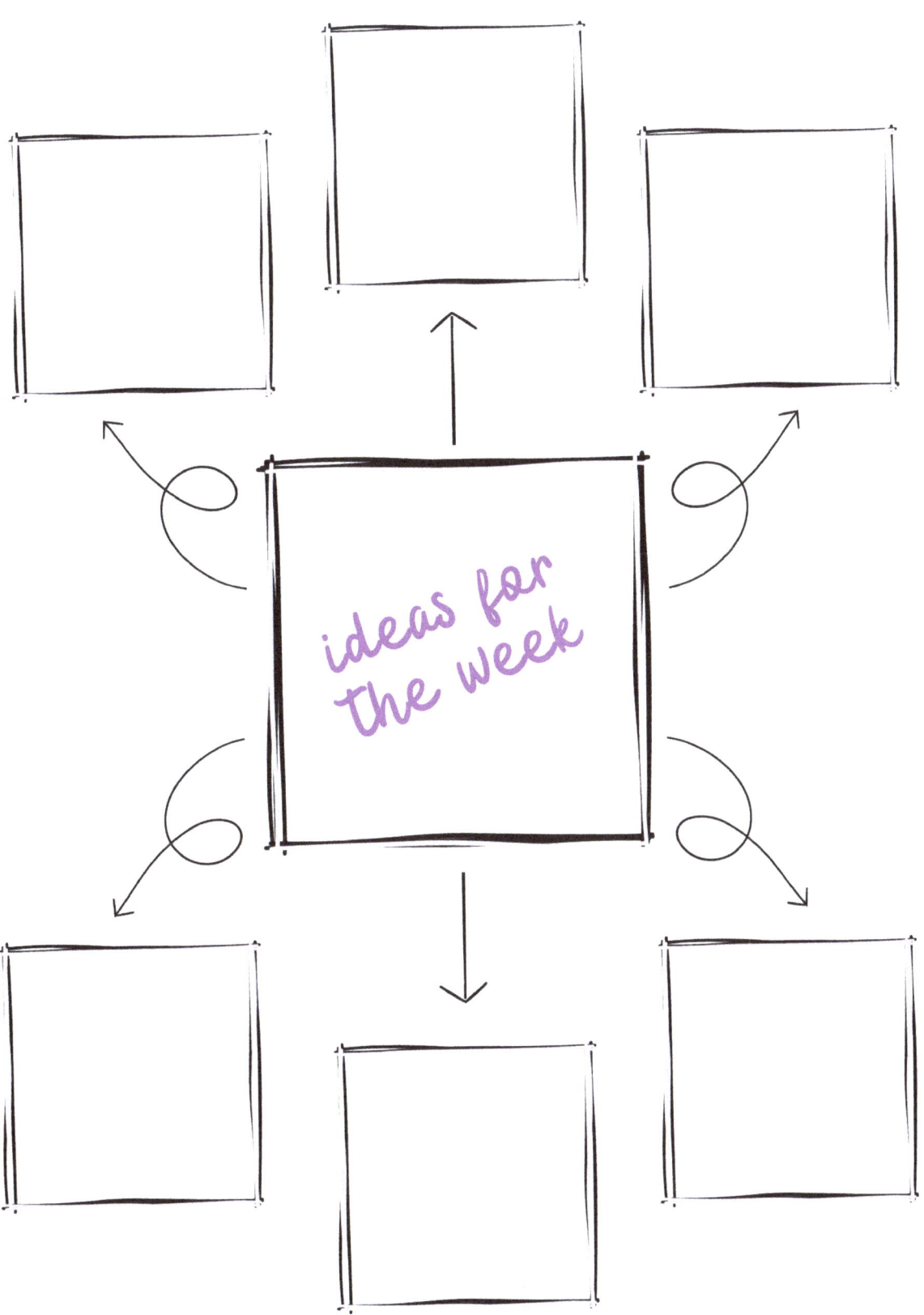

ideas for the week

Important Contacts

Contact 1

Name

Phone

Email

Address

Contact 2

Name

Phone

Email

Address

Contact 3

Name

Phone

Email

Address

Contact 4

Name

Phone

Email

Address

Contact 5

Name

Phone

Email

Address

Contact 6

Name

Phone

Email

Address

Contact 7

Name

Phone

Email

Address

Contact 8

Name

Phone

Email

Address

Important Contacts

Contact 9

Name

Phone

Email

Address

Contact 10

Name

Phone

Email

Address

Contact 11

Name

Phone

Email

Address

Contact 12

Name

Phone

Email

Address

Contact 13

Name

Phone

Email

Address

Contact 14

Name

Phone

Email

Address

Contact 15

Name

Phone

Email

Address

Contact 16

Name

Phone

Email

Address

Section 4
My God-given Purpose Check-in

Now, that you have been doing what you are called to do. What pieces of your plan need to be updated and why?

What have you accomplish thus far?

What lessons have you learned during this process? How can you improve moving forward?

Woman of Purpose

Clothed in strength and dignity

Kissed by light

Covered in healing

Stretched wide like the wings of an eagle

She is like no other

Christ grown

Dipped in refreshing water

Made anew

A soul of abundance

Chosen for more

I am She

I am a Woman of Purpose

Dr. Shavon Leach

I am a Woman Of Purpose.

How does this make you feel?

What does this mean to you?

How has this affirmation and process transformed you?

Letter To Myself

Hey Woman Of Purpose

You have reached the end of your Woman of Purpose journal.

I pray that this journey has been filled with powerful

realizations that will carry you into your future.

You are powerful!

You were created to leave a lasting impact. Continue to grow.

Someone is waiting on your God-given impact.

Forever Open

www.ingramcontent.com/pod-product-compliance
Lightning Source LLC
Chambersburg PA
CBHW041119120626
46547CB00019B/2766